AF489937

Messages for the Wounded by Betrayal

Wisdom from the other side of pain

Helen Tower

Dear sibling in pain,

You are responsible only for your own recovery. The betrayal by someone you trusted and maybe built a life or a business with, has NOTHING to do with you. It is 100% the betrayer's choice.

The pain is real, though, and you are left to deal with the consequences. Start from healing yourself.

I have compiled quotes that have helped others who were facing the aftermath of betrayal with me. You can come out the other side of pain and feel joy again.

Love,

Helen Tower

About this book

Helen Tower is the pen name chosen by the author to be able to communicate hope to people who, like her, have been betrayed by a loved one.

It is important to understand why and how betrayal is a painful loss that shakes the foundations on which we build our life.

Whether you have been betrayed by a spouse, a parent, a business partner, a sibling or a friend, the wound can be deep, especially if you were all in and vulnerable in the relationship.

It is important to grieve the loss of trust in an individual or an institution. Even if you are not aware, your brain changes and adapts to the trauma caused by betrayal.

This book is a compilation of wisdom nuggets shared by the author and her tribe of betrayed spouses who supported each other during more than three years.

They appear in no particular order. You can open any page at random when you want to receive a message during your path to recovery.

Healing from betrayal is possible. You will learn to trust again.

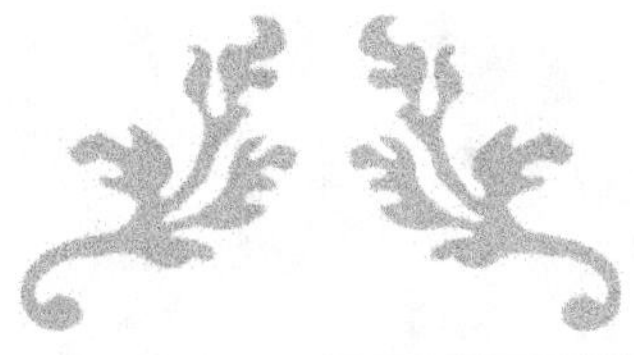

Messages from the other side of pain

Read in any order

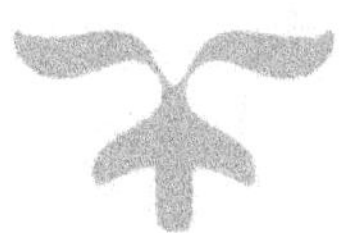

Long-term relationships
will be damaged at some
point. It is normal to have
to do repair work. The fairy
tale we are told as kids is a
lie. There is no living
happily ever after without
doing the work.

Understanding trauma is key for recovering from betrayal. Emergency neurological pathways take over when what we thought was certain is no more. You must protect your body from the effects of intense stress.

Self love is not only about pampering yourself. It is mainly about self-compassion. Be kind to yourself. You are doing your best. It's okay to take a break from the hard work of recovering from betrayal.

Even if the betrayer leaves the partnership, make sure you learn from the experience. We are all imperfect humans with our own patterns and we interpret the world differently.

Communication
skills are sharpened
when recovering
from betrayal. We
must learn to listen
to ourselves and pay
attention to how we
express our needs.

Trust, love and
friendship are all
redefined as we
recover from the
pain of betrayal. We
learn to be
responsible for our
own wellbeing.

In case of doubt as
to what to do next,
look inwards. Being
honest with
ourselves is the first
step in the right
direction.

Don't let anyone underestimate your pain. If it hurts it must be addressed. Healing means you will not be transmitting the pain to those around you.

If you wonder "Why
me?", know that this
thought will fade away.
One day you will start
enjoying life again.

Find a private and efficient outlet for your pain. Journaling is a great way to organize your thoughts and feelings without burdening those around you.

The trauma from betrayal requires long term empathy. It can be found in people who are going through the same pain. You can find your tribe anonymously on social platforms.

Make sure you find a
safe way to
communicate your
pain. A community of
betrayed people
offers the support
you need. You cannot
do it alone.

Only you will decide when to stop feeling the victim. One day you will say "I want to feel joy again". That's how you realize that it is up to you to do more of what makes you happy.

Include fun activities in your program. You are the adult responsible for organizing your own life. There are free activities you can do. It's not a matter of money.

Revenge brings havoc to your life instead of the peace you so much seek after the trauma of betrayal.

One day you will be
ready to risk being in a
partnership again. Keep
your values intact. After
betrayal it is even more
important to remain
true to yourself.

Use the anger that you feel
as a force to impulse your
self-love and healing. You
cannot control what others
do or did. You can only take
the reins of your own path
to recovery. You can come
out of this pain a stronger
person.

Nothing can undo the fact that someone you trusted chose to betray you. What you can do is decide to leave it in the past where it belongs and learn to live with your reality now.

You are not responsible
for the betrayer's
choices. There was
nothing you could have
done differently to
prevent deceit. Take care
of your wounds. Healing
is possible.

Were you born a warrior or a people pleaser? You inherit traumas from your ancestors you are not even aware of. You can learn to speak up and ask for your needs or stop fighting other people's battles.

Healing is not linear. There
are good days and bad days.
Keep loving yourself, do
more of what makes you
happy and, gradually, the
better days will outnumber
the painful ones.

Betrayal does not come with a switch to stop loving the betrayer. The heartache is real. Give yourself permission to acknowledge this. It is the first step towards recovery.

If the betrayer is
remorseful and willing
to make amends, you
can give the
relationship you had
together ONE chance.
It is an act of self-love
from you to you.

Place your hand on you
heart and breathe
deeply into it. This
synchronizes it with
your brain and allows
you to get in touch
with your true feelings.

Whatever you are feeling is okay. Heartbreak is painful and any of the grief stages can be present at any point in time: anger, denial, sadness, bargaining or acceptance.

Allow yourself to stay
present and flow. Let
go of the need to want
for others to change. It
is not in your power.
Focus on what you can
do to get closer to
where you want to be.

Discovering the betrayal means the secret is out. The betrayer stops hiding and the betrayed confirms their suspicion. The path to recovery starts.

Trauma can be cured by empowering yourself. Start doing something you enjoy that you can finish quickly. Small accomplishments help build your self-confidence and rewire your brain away from the pain of the betrayal.

Never stop learning. You have already survived betrayal. You now know the sun will rise again tomorrow.

Healing takes time. Be patient. One day, the uncontrolled thoughts will become less frequent and you will be able to create good memories again.

Those who lied to you
do not deserve your
attention. They thrive
on other people's
energy. Purposely turn
your focus on to
something productive.

Simple chores that you
enjoy can have a huge
impact on you mental
health. The instant
gratification of smelling a
beautiful flower or
holding a warm cup of
tea are healing and
grounding.

Don't let the toxicity
of a grudge poison
your inner world. Own
your peace. Carry on
without this
predicament.

Running away from the
pain will not make it
disappear. You need to
do the work to heal or it
will follow you wherever
you go and into new
relationships.

Transform the pain
into strength. You will
become a wiser
person as you grow.

Trauma is caused when
our relationships break
down. Take good care
of yourself. Your body
needs it.

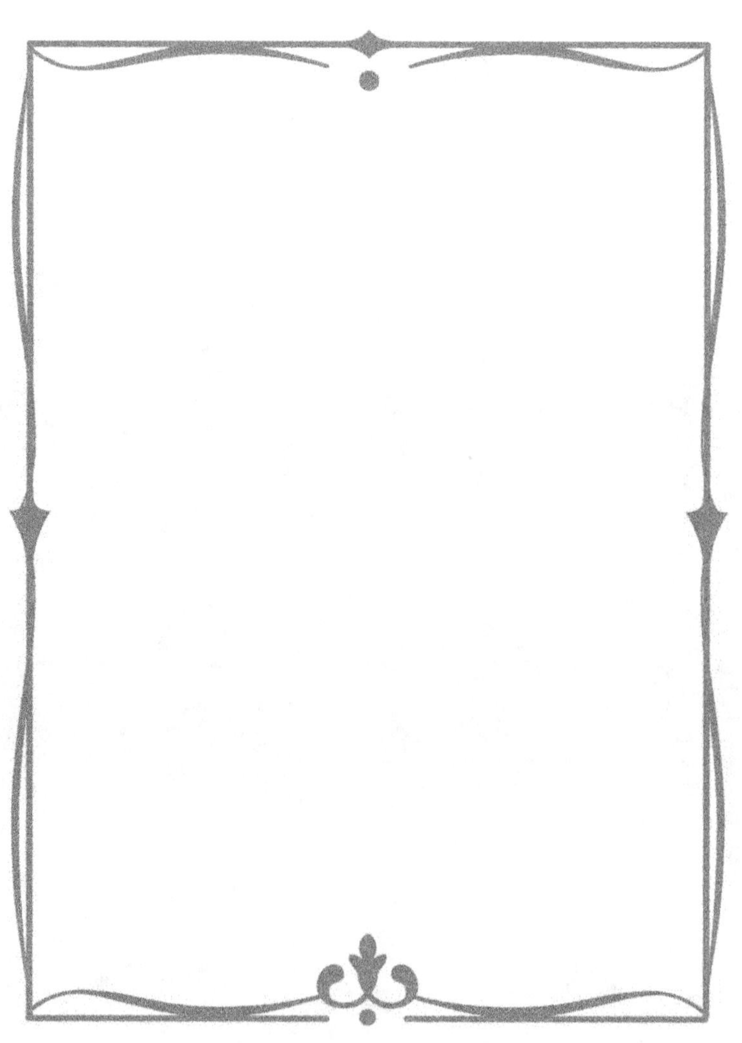

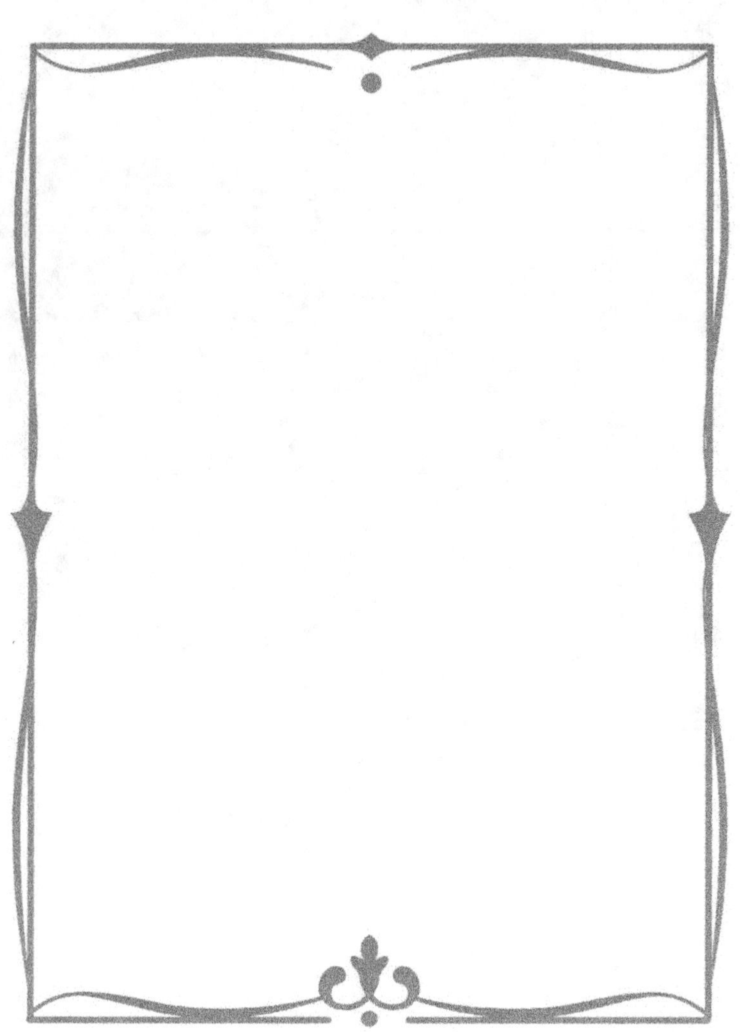

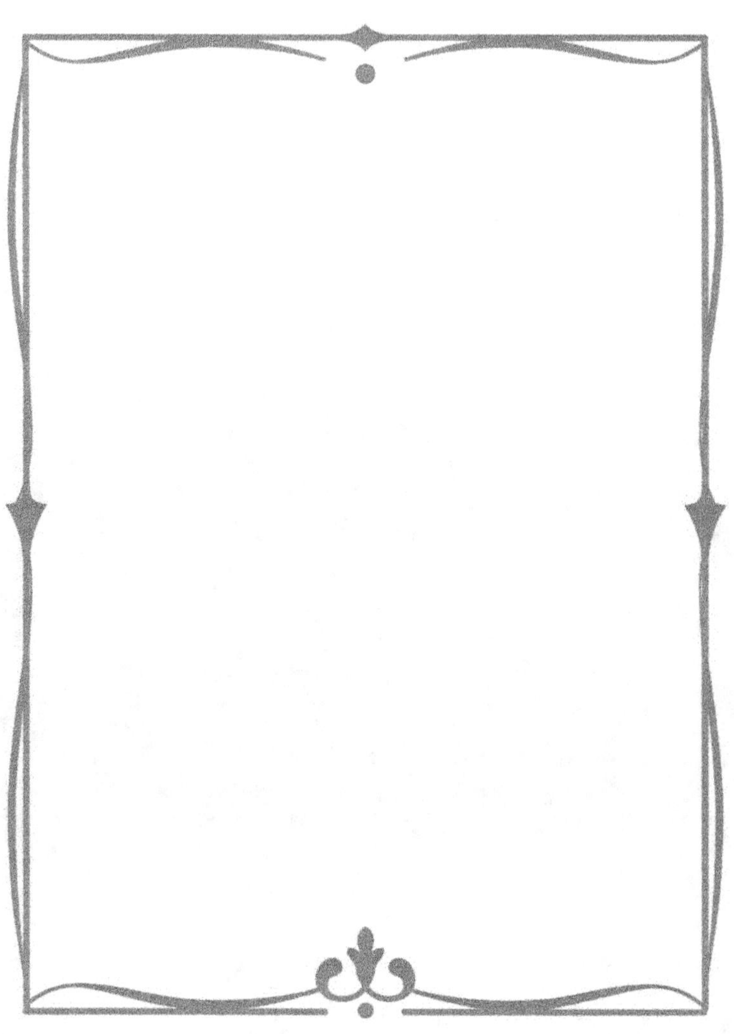

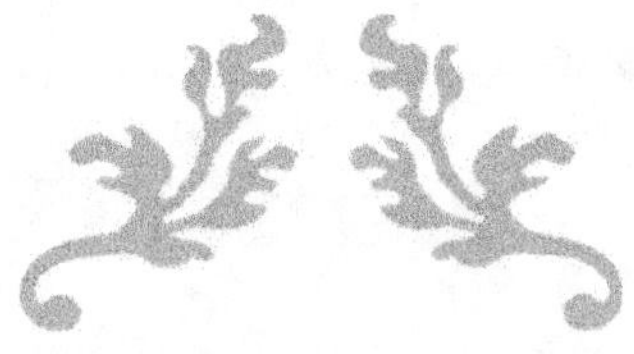

What to do when you are not feeling strong

Ideas

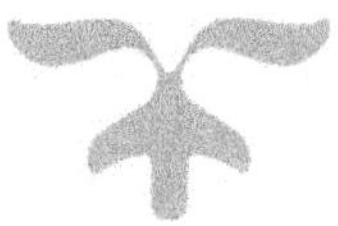

Breathe and feel the air going in and out of your lungs

Rest by
allowing
yourself just
to feel the
feelings

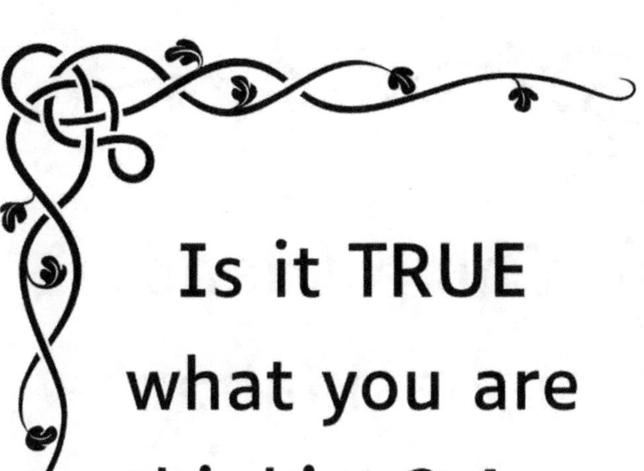

Is it TRUE what you are thinking? Are you sure it is true?

Call a friend
and ask about
their life. No
need to talk
about you.

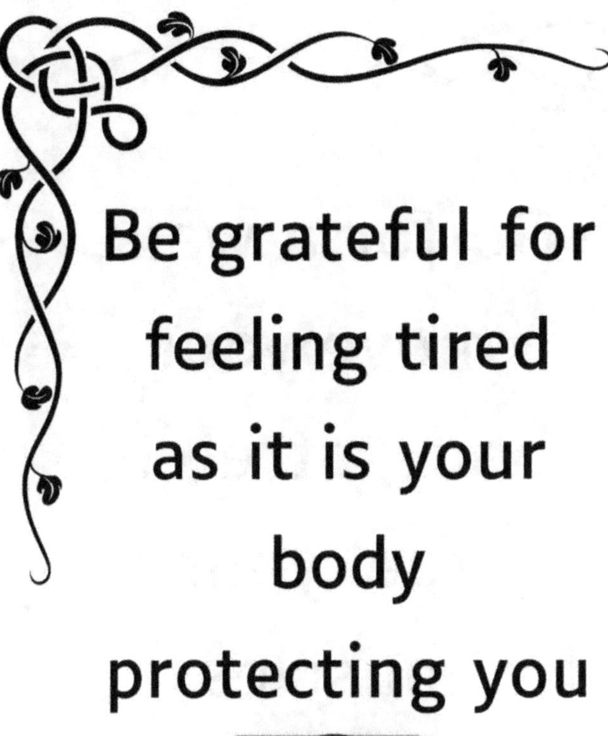

Be grateful for
feeling tired
as it is your
body
protecting you

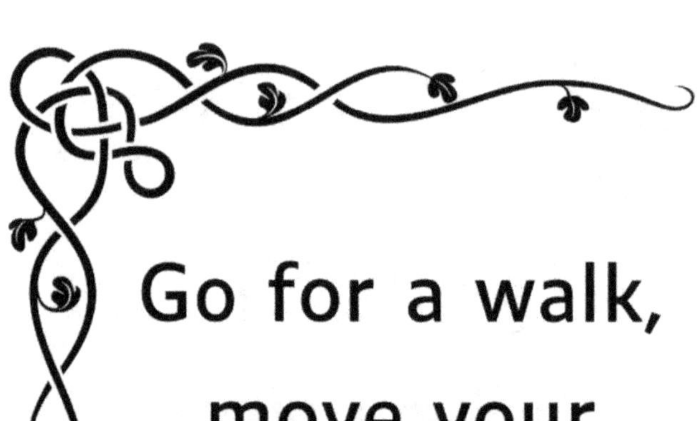

Go for a walk, move your body, stretch, feel your muscles.

Watch a
sketch you
enjoy.

Listen to
music that will
take you to
times before
the betrayal

Look at
photos from
activities that
have nothing
to do with it

Prepare some comfort food

Take a hot
bath or
shower

Light some
scent candles
or sticks

Say no to

what doesn't

make you

happy

Lakes help
you look
inwards with
compassion

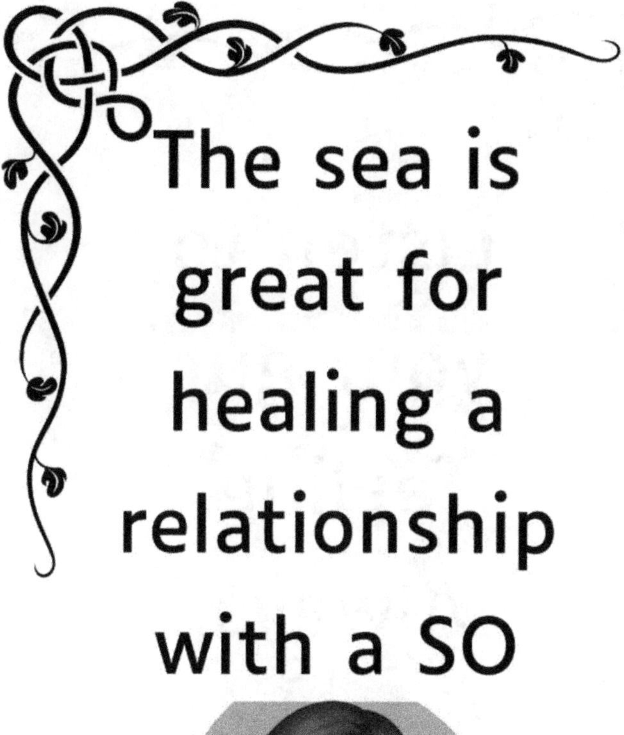

The sea is
great for
healing a
relationship
with a SO

Listen to

your gut

feeling.

Always.

Seek medical attention if you are not well.

Go for a
walk in
nature

Answer some questions

How are you feeling today?

Sit with the feeling, don't fight it. It will stay with you and leave sooner if you do not resist it.

What comes to mind? Write freely in the space below:

The pages that follow are for you to write
or to draw whatever comes to mind.

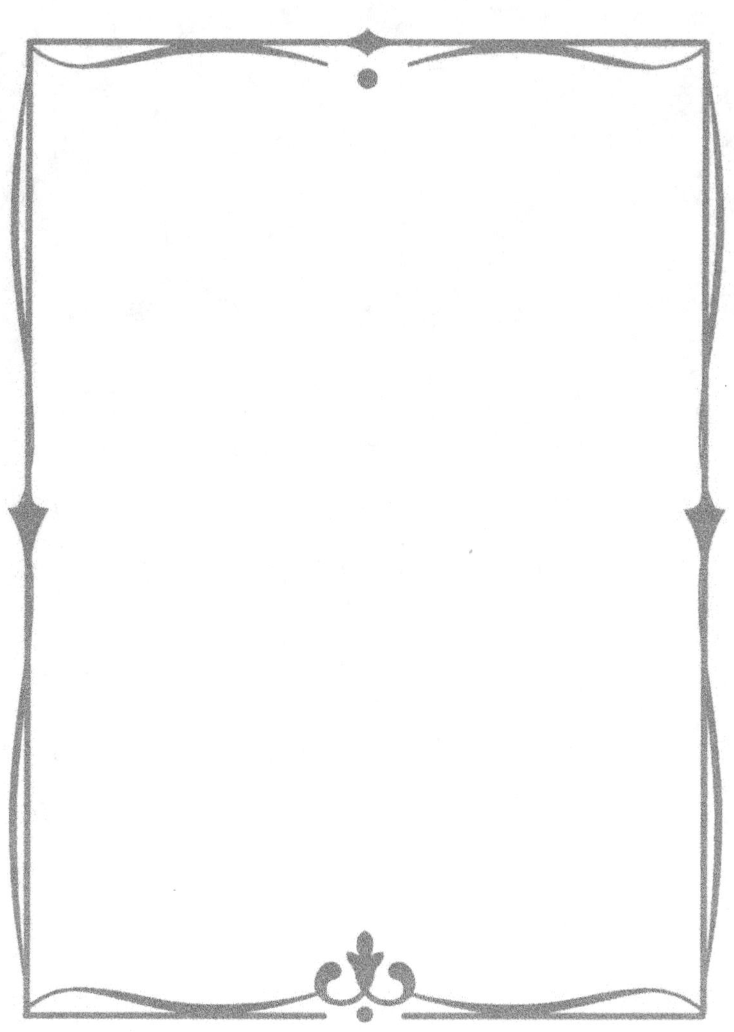

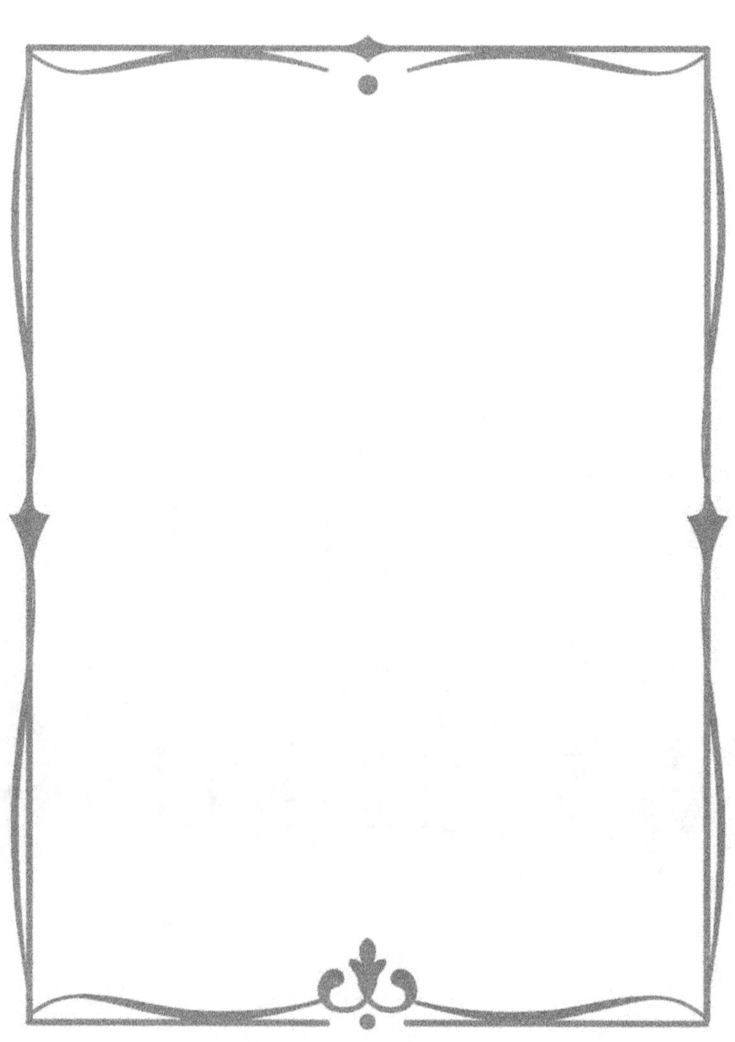

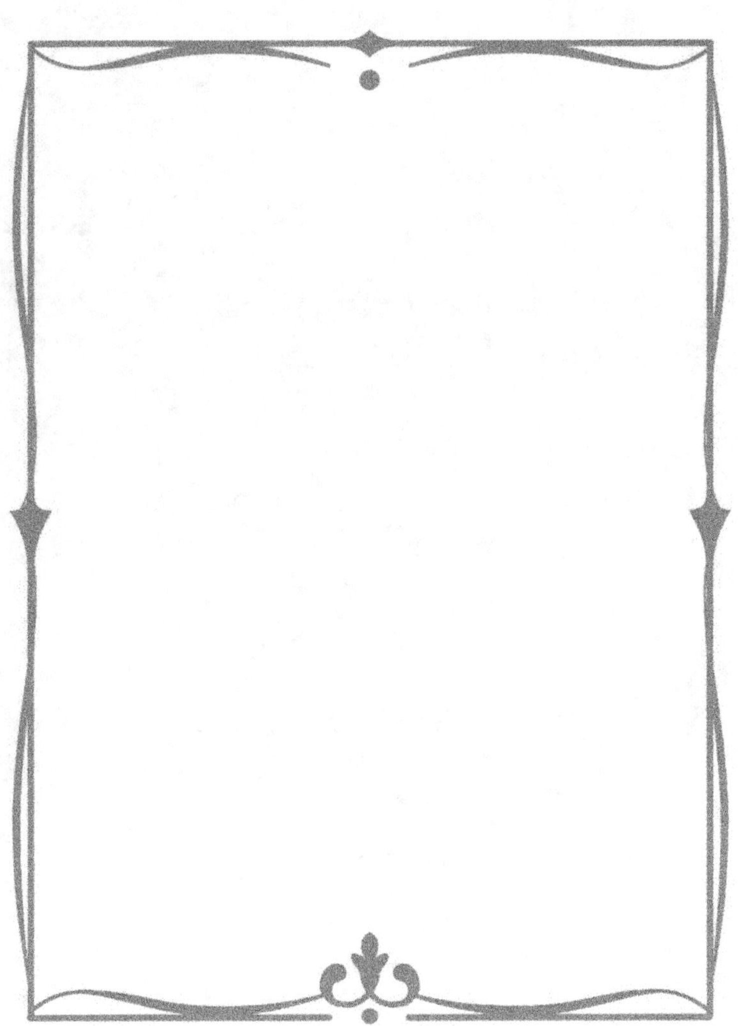

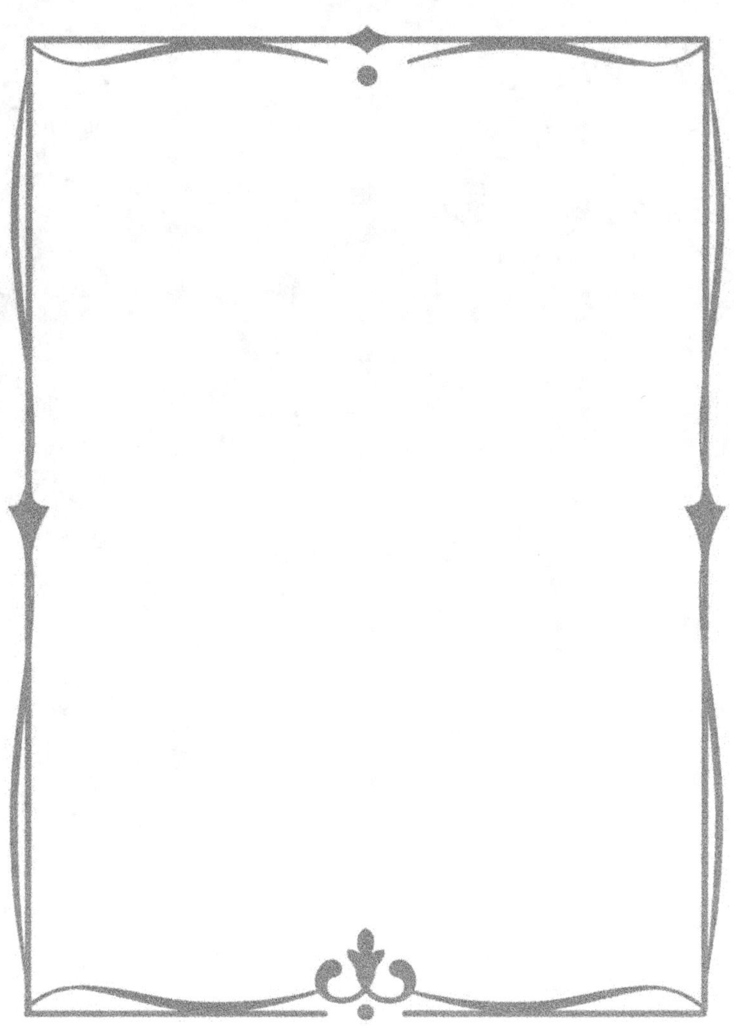

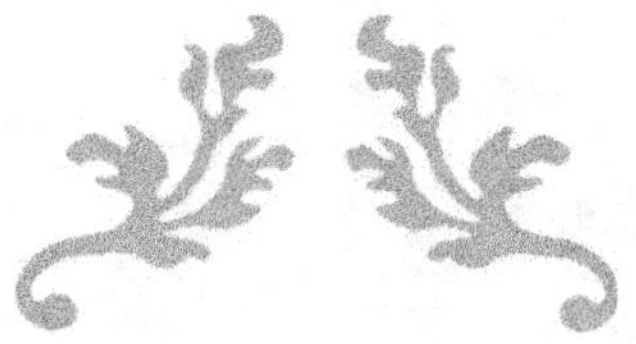

Doubt

A poem

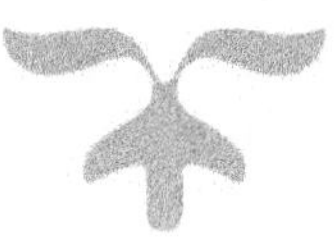

When you look at their behaviour,
Can you tell
What's real or not?

You can see the moving mouth
articulating the words.

Are they saying what they must
Or are they talking from the heart?

Sometimes children learn from small
To lie and lie and then once more.

They depend on it for real,
to protect their sense of self.

They think their carers won't look after them
shall they honestly speak.
So they twist, praise and lie
About what their elders want to hear.

Machiavellians in the making,
Triggered by fear
Sometimes real, sometimes not,
That in their hearts and souls
Protects them from bad memories
Or real danger.

And they grow being polite,
Lying, thanking just for that.

Not because they mean a word.

So how can someone who believed,
Who says thank you, please and so
'Cause they mean it really well,
Know when a person who's now bare
Showing lies that caused despair,
Tell the truth or just peruse
Some old trick they learned as children
To get away, get by or win?

There's no way
For now we know
After betrayal of any sort
That the only one we trust
Is our lonely standing self.

Even that we must protect
For if we lie about our doubt
To protect, care or whatever,
We will cross the line of fear
That will blur what's real and clear.

Let the doubt out, I say,
Let the betrayer know about it
Even if pain it causes.

It is good for your sanity
And a warning to the other party.
If he's using his technique

He's reminded of the dangers
Of a second lie unfolding.

And to you, my wounded soul,
I say go, tune up and grow.
This new pattern you're aware of
Shall protect you from life's evil.

For beside pure souls,
There are frightened liars
Who sought deceit over surrender
And can't help but to repeat
Once they're now not so tender.

Helen Tower

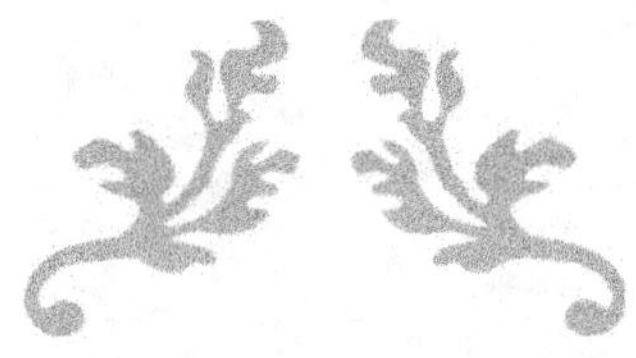

Ode to the healed female

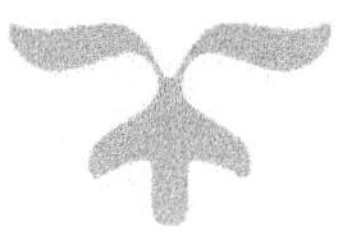

You have now freed yourself
and all of your female
ancestors. Your daughter and
granddaughters have been
healed and can stand on their
own two feet. You are not
afraid of not being loved
anymore. You have understood
where the secret lays. You go,
girl!

About the author

Helen Tower has published two books about her recovery path from the infidelity of her husband of twenty-two years. They are available on Amazon.com, both on digital and paperback editions.

She has a blog, SailingThroughInfidelity.blogspot.com and a podcast, Sailing Infidelity, available on most audio platforms.

You can connect with Helen on Twitter as @SailingInfidel1, Instagram @HelenTowerStayCalm and Facebook @HelenTowerAuthor

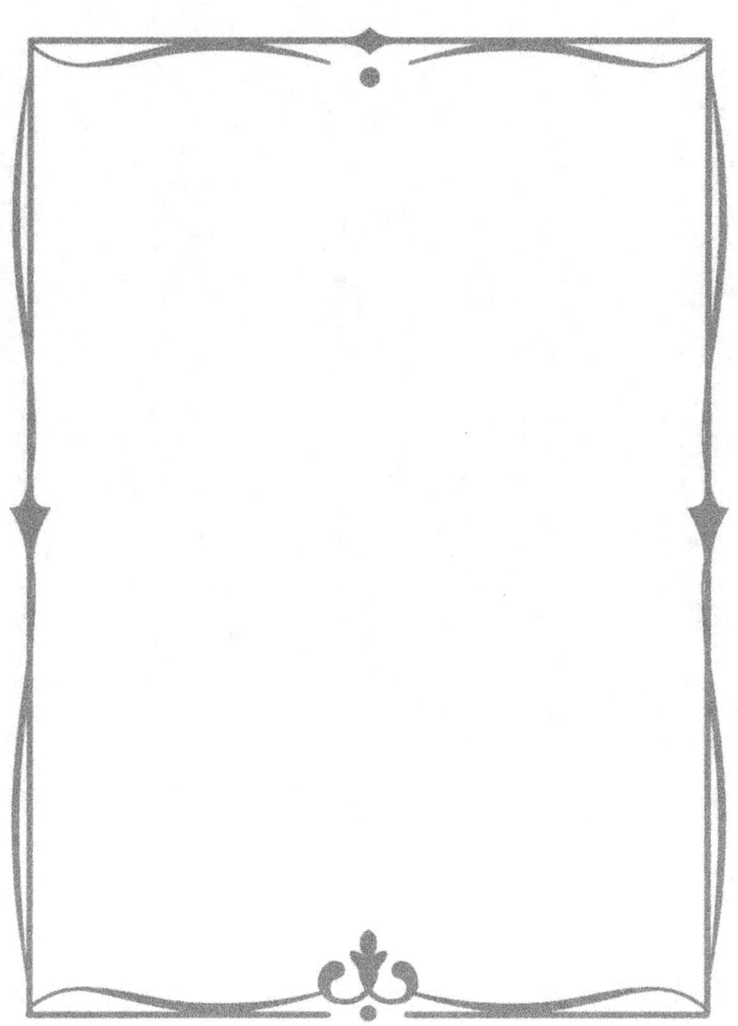

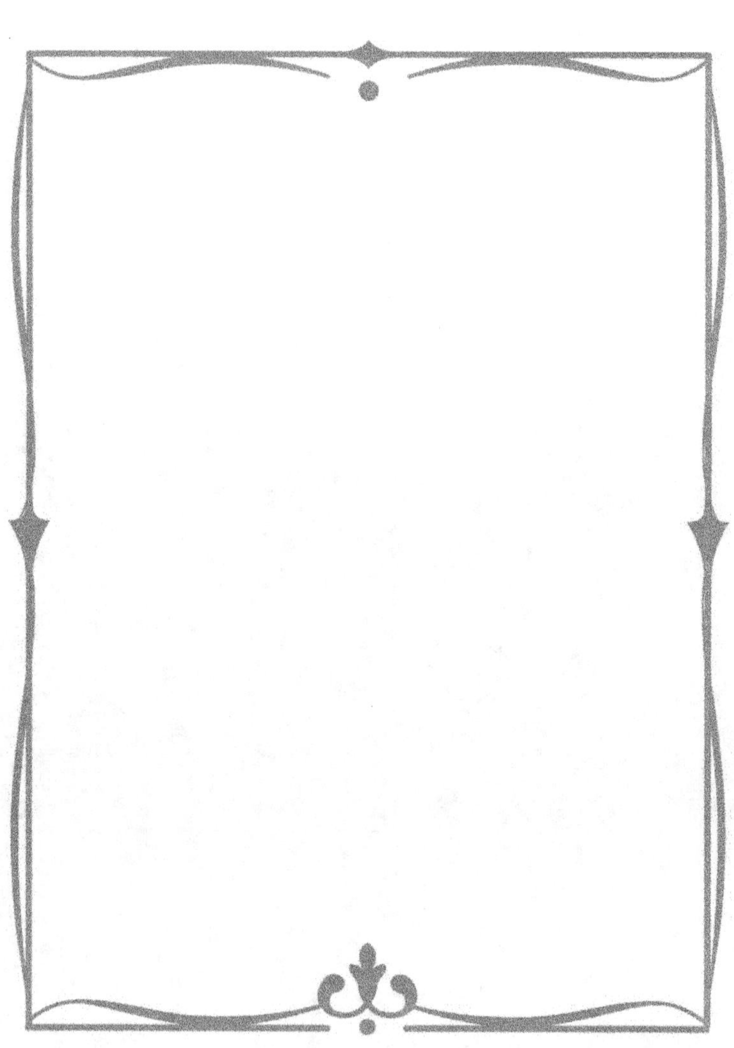